Source of Inspiration

Vol. IV

Inspirational Poems
From: *Source of Inspiration*

Website: www.patcegan.wordpress.com

Copyright © 2017 Patricia E. Cegan

All rights reserved. No part of this publication may be used for commercial gain. However, readers may reproduce and distribute for the sole purpose of sharing the inspiration of these Source poems. Should you wish to use this series of inspirational poetry for fund raising purposes for charitable causes, please contact Ms. Cegan at the email address below.

Published by:

1Creator Publishing, USA

E-mail: patcegan@hotmail.com

ISBN 10: 0-99-75128-2-2

Illustrations: by Pat Cegan Please note that the cover illustration is made from mushroom prints that Pat gathered in the beautiful floresta surrounding her cabin.

Table of Contents

MOON 1

SEED SOWER 2

THE COCOON 2

THE STREAM 3

THE SEA 3

FOOLS IN CHARGE 4

JUST ASK 4

GOD'S MIRROR 5

RIDE THE WIND 6

BROKEN STONES 6

WHAT THE EAGLE SEES 7

THE VASTNESS WITHIN 7

THE EAGLE 8

WHAT I'M NOT 8

GOD'S GLORY 9

TALKING WITH GOD 10

MUSIC EVERYWHERE 11

HOW LONG? 12

VISIT YOURSELF 13

CHILD OF NOW 13

COMING BACK	14
SHY	14
THE BAG	15
GRATITUDE #5	15
SOMETHING FOR NOTHING	16
CARTOON ILLUSION	16
GOLDEN BASKETS	17
GRATITUDE #6	18
MY BUBBLE	18
TRAIN TO WHERE?	19
ALREADY BEEN	19
WHO IS WEALTHY?	20
ONCE A BULLY	20
SPRING ECSTASY	21
PRETTY?	21
SOUL SILENCE	22
GRATITUDE #7	22
LIFE REVEALED	23
WHAT'S WITHIN	23
GIFT OF INSOMNIA	24
PROMISES	24

TRANSPARENT MAN	24
CYCLES	25
THINK AGAIN	26
THE PATIENCE OF GOD	27
NO SECRETS	28
CLOAK OF HELPLESSNESS	29
COUNTING LEAVES	29
MONK'S WINE	30
GRATITUDE #8	31
A RAMBLING FOOL	31
ONE BY ONE	32
VISION WITHOUT EYES	33
EVERYWHERE	34
ALL CHILDREN	35
KNOWLEDGE IS NOT WISDOM	35
FOOL'S PLAY	36
THE PERFECT PEAR	36
THE BEGGAR AND DOG	37
WAR	37
MY PIECE OF LAND	39
THE IMPOSSIBLE	41

SCIENCE AND MYSTICISM	42
THE CANDLE	43
HELPING	43
A MOMENT IN TIME	43
IN ITS TIME	44
PATTERNS IN NATURE	45
ABSOLUTE TRUTHS	46
THE SILENT BREATH	47
YARD SALE JUNK	48
WHAT IF?	49
POWER	50
OUR FAMILY	52
WAKE-UP CALL	52
ONE TINY FLOWER	53
OUR DEFECTS	53
LOVE BEACON	54
MATHEMATICS OF LOVE	54
COURAGE	54
PUZZLE OF LIFE	55
REALITY MIRRORS ITSELF	56
MANIFESTING LIFE #1	57

YOUR MISSION	57
MANIFESTING LIFE #2	58
LOTUS	59
YOUR SECRET SIN	59
THAT MAN	60
THE TAKERS	61
MANIFESTING LIFE #3	62
PROPHECY #3 – TIME JUMPERS	62
ME?	64
4X4'S	64
HOPE	65
FAITH AND HOPE	65
SIN	66
PROPHECY #4 – BALANCE	66
OUR ANGRY MOTHER	67
HOW PRECIOUS YOUR LOVE	68
GRACE	68
COMPLIMENTS	69
THE BUGLE	69
THE AXE	70
YOUR WORDS, MY PEN	71

GOLDEN WHEAT	71
CROOKED ROAD	72
COCK'S CROW	73
ROCKING CHAIR	74
MANIFESTING LIFE #4	75
GOD THINKS OF EVERYTHING	75
ENDURANCE	76
LOVING WORDS	76
ABSOLUTION	76
FALSE TEACHERS	77
RECIPROCAL	77
FLAME OF LIGHT	78
JOYOUSLY SAD	78
BEGGAR'S BOWL	79
CALL OF THE SIREN	80
DRUNK WITH LOVE	80
THE ROCK OF GOD	81
SILENT POEM	82
LONGING	82
CONSUMED	83
ENDLESS WORDS	84

ONLY A SHADOW	84
RAZOR'S EDGE	85
THE LOTTERY	86
MADLY SERENE	87
MY PEN KNOWS	87
HOLLOW	88
THE THIRSTY FISH	89
BECOME THE SKY	90
EMPTY	90
BOUND BY FEAR	91
TREE OF RESPECT	92
GOD?	93
P	93
THE BALLERINA	94
CHANGE	95
THE VESSEL	95
BECOME ALL	96
MY ENEMY?	96
IN LOVE WITH LOVE	96
WHAT IT IS	97
FINDING PEARLS	98

WHAT IS LIFE? 98

WEAVING MOONBEAMS 99

JUST BEING 100

SITTING IN THE SUN 100

GOOD ENOUGH 100

I AM LIGHT 101

IN A TIME BEFORE 102

OUR ADDICTIONS 102

FOLLOW THE LIGHT 103

OUR STRENGTH 104

THE SECRET OF LIFE 104

JUST GOD 104

A WISE ONE 105

LIVE YOUR LIFE 105

IRONY OF INSPIRATION 106

ROSEBUD 106

WHY KISS? 107

SUGAR CANE 107

UNION 108

WORLD OF FOOLS 109

RICH OR POOR? 109

LIGHT I CANNOT SEE	110
THE GARDEN	111
PIT OF MADNESS	111
WONDER OF LOVE	112
LOVE ENDURES	112
COMPLAINTS	112
FLYING	113
SPIRITUAL ARROGANCE	113
A SINGLE DROP	114
POPPY PROMISES	114
CO-CREATORS OF LIGHT	115
JUST ONE NOTE	115
SLICE OF PIE	115
CAT'S PURR	116
ILLUSIONS	116
LOVE OR NOT	116
WHAT YOU WANT	117
OCEAN MUSIC	117
MY WORST HABIT	118
NO NEED OF GRACE	119
WHIRLPOOLS	120

WHAT EXISTS?	121
THE SKEPTIC	121
THAT WHICH YOU ARE	122
KNOWLEDGE TO WISDOM	123
A NUT OF TRUTH	123
CRY MORE	124
A WAVE	125
OTHER WORLDS?	125
THE POND	126
LOVE'S SANCTUARY	126
MY STAR	127
YOUR INTUITION	127
TRAINS	128
SOUL	129
RIGHT HERE	129
THRONE OF CONTEMPLATION	129
WEAVING MOONBEAMS	130
ONLY WITH YOU	130
LUMBER JACKS	131
A SURGE	132
YOUR TROPHY	132

CHORD OF LONGING	133
HOLDING TRUTH	134
LET GO	135
PURE WATER	135
THE THRONE	136
EVERYWHERE	137
A MOTE	137
HIDING IN SHADOWS	138
TRUST IN THE LORD	138
GOD IS	139
FREEDOM OF LIGHT	139
LANGUAGE OF LOVE	140
SO SIMPLE	141
CHOOSING	141
MANY WAYS	142
SHARED WORRY	142
BE YOU	143
TIMBER!	143
ICE CREAM CONE	144
WHO ARE YOU?	144
AWAKE, YET ASLEEP	145

WHICH?	146
CAN'T DECIDE	146
RICH MAN	147
ONE OR TWO?	147
AT LAST	148
SOON	148
JUMPIN' AND A HOPPIN'	149
ARK OF MYSTERY	149
THE STALLION	150
A PURPLE FEATHER	150
DIAMONDS OF LOVE	151
TRAPPED	151
IMPOLITE	152
WALK AWAY	152
TO NO AVAIL	153
LOVE TO TALK	154
DON'T ASK	154
THE SAME	155
SO IMPATIENT	155
THIS LOVE	156
FEEDING THE FLAME	157

PRIVATE HINTS	158
EMPTY	159
LEARNING PATIENCE	159
THE DRUM	159
THERE'S ONLY LOVE	160
INFINITE	160
COMING HOME	161
NO GREEN	161
MORE POETRY	162
COUNTING TIME	162
GOING AWAY PARTY	163
LITTLE PUFF	164
FILLED WITH POETRY	164
A MELODY	165
CRITTER SALAD	166
A DROP	166
WHAT DID YOU SAY?	166
NOPE!	167
CLOSER TO GOD	167
ALREADY ARE	168
CIRCLE OF DARKNESS	169

THE WHISPERER	169
DIVIDING LINE	170
THE GIFT OF PAIN	170
CELESTIAL MUSIC	170
THE SAME	171
BELIEFS	172
GOD IS	172
LIES IN LAYERS	173
WHAT IS SPIRITUALITY?	173
NOTHING MORE	174
INSIDE OF WALLS	175
AND THEN THERE IS	175
I EXIST	176
POWER OF INTENTION	176
FACE	177
FACE2	177
FACE3	177
FACE4	177
CALLING FORTH	178
DISCO QUEEN	178
CHILDHOOD STORIES	179

FINGER AND THUMB 179

U R 180

TRUE SERENITY 180

HAVING FUN 180

BIRD BLESSINGS 181

A DELICACY 181

ME 181

EXCELLENCE 182

JUST A MOMENT 182

NO MORE DRAMA 183

GIVING THANKS 183

FOREVER FRIEND 183

HIDING 184

NO PLANS 184

ONLY ME 185

NO MORE JOURNEYS 185

NEW TEACHER 186

DRINKING 186

WONDROUS IS SHE 187

ANTICIPATION 188

MAKE ME LAUGH 189

NO JAIL	189
CLATTER CHATTER	190
NO PROOF NEEDED	190
DEVOURING LIFE	191
AWE	191
THE CONNOISSEUR	191
MORE AND MORE	192
NOT YET	192
VANILLA ME	193
JUST A GAME	193
WHERE IS HOME?	194
UPSIDE DOWN	194
FOOTSTEPS	194
ICING ON THE CAKE	195
PAPER AIRPLANE	196
ALL DAY SUCKER	196
NO SHOULDS	196
TREAD WITH CARE	197
DON'T JUST TAKE	197
INTO THE HOLE	198
DON'T BOTHER	198

THE SWING 199

SNOW DROPS 199

CAT IN A HAT 200

THE RUM BUM 200

DECIDING 200

BEAUTIFUL 201

Moon

The full moon is speechless
a silent sphere of cold light
even the stars twinkle
but not the moon.

Oh, it can wax and wane
even change color
but it cannot tell you
what's on the other side.

Ambiguous is the moon
neither silk nor coarse linen
full of changing smiles
her name has been erased
now no one knows who she is.

Only that sometimes
she exists
other times
she does not.

Seed Sower

I am a planter of seeds.
What comes will be long after I'm gone.
Some plant flowers; others plant weeds.
I am a planter of seeds.
Wherever you go, leave footprints of joy
Fill the air around with the fragrance of love.
I am a planter of seeds.
What comes will be long after I'm gone.

The Cocoon

Inside my cocoon
a transformation is going on.
I am leaving behind who I was
with the process of becoming
moth of the night
butterfly of the day
or perhaps a dragon
full of mystery.

Who is the creature?
A changeling
full of knowing
a deviate from the norm
or one of many who are
arriving to save the world?

Oh, I'm changing
you may not think so
but I am
stand by to be surprised
soon all will be revealed.

The Stream

Standing in the stream
wailing for water
to quench your thirst.
God is everywhere
you foolish one
just open your mouth
and drink.

The Sea

Searching
books, gurus, religion
endless questions
with no answers.
I am drowning
while asking
where is the sea?

Fools in Charge

How we love
to run and hide
leaving fools in charge
then complain
about the disasters
they make.

Take charge.
If you must live

with mistakes
let them at least
be your own.

Just Ask

God knows your helplessness
He stands ready to aid you.
Oh how you suffer
but do not call for Him.

Is it pride that keeps
you bound to your woe?
I say, "Open the gates.
Let God's mercy flood in."

Still you suffer in your
stubbornness, not sure
there is a God
Just a waste of time to call.

More sorrow comes
and heaps
upon your head.

Will you drown in your
sea of sin while a life boat
waits nearby?
Let go of your disbelief
before it drags you down.
Take His hand
He's waiting to
when you do.

God's Mirror

   I am God's mirror
   Polished to a high shine
   reflecting His love
   throughout eternity.

   When you look at me
   you'll see God's love
   reflected back to you
   then you'll be blessed
  and become His mirror, too.

Ride the Wind

    The wind blows
  the litter of greed, lust, hate
  making whirlwinds of woe.
   You need not stay
  in this storm, Dear Ones.
  You need only step aside
   unless, of course
  you prefer to ride the wind.

Broken Stones

Let broken stones
be your gold
for you've no need of either.
What is most treasured
is God's love
and that He gives
to those with the humility
to ask.

What the Eagle Sees

A man sits
on a mountain top
gazing as far as
he can see.
An eagle flies by
and asks, What are you
looking for? God, the man
replies. Have you seen him?
Indeed, I have
the eagle replied
when I first looked
at thee.

The Vastness Within

There is a vastness within
that terrifies us with
its enormity. We see it
as a pit of vipers rather
than the haven it is.
Oh foolish one
let go and sink
within. Then open
your eyes and see
that death and life
are the same thing
circling into eternity.

The Eagle

Eagle
soaring, riding the currents
all seeing eyes of God
his nobility is plain to see
Symbol of fidelity

What I'm Not

I am not black or white
or any other color or creed.
I am not what I wear
or where I work.
Nothing of this world
can define me.

What I am is a spark
of the Light of the Divine
and you are, too.
We can ignore this
or expand it
through intention
service and love.
Either way
the Light remains true.

God's Glory

Sometimes I feel lost
as if I were walking
at night and the stars
and moon blinked off.

The dark surrounds me
leaving me disoriented
not knowing up or down
east or west
suspended am I
afraid to move
all dreaded possibilities
hovering nearby.
Then I hear a sweet voice
within begin to sing
a childhood refrain
"This little light of mine
I'm going to let it shine."
And as I joined in
one by one

my fears disappeared
until the sky is filled
with God's glory
and so am I.

Talking With God

It may seem that
I'm talking to myself
muttering here and there
but actually, I have
a running dialogue
with God, back and forth
we go.

If you call me
and I don't respond
I'm listening to the Lord.
You young people call me crazy
but it's because you
have not learned
how to talk with God
throughout your day
instead of set times
to pray which to me
is talking *at* God
instead of with Him.

But, what do I know
a crazy old woman
living in the floresta
with God her constant
companion?

Music Everywhere

Everything is music
to he who has joy
in his heart
lilting breezes
flowers nodding
streams cascading
claps of thunder
the tympani drum of God.

Let your world be filled
with joyous melodies
even the clouds
are filled with misty songs.

How Long?

How long will you
wait for me, God?
As long as it takes
replies He.

Would I have such
patience, I wonder.
So many times
harsh words I've spoken
when what was needed
was love.

Visit Yourself

Do you visit yourself
faithfully, inquiring
how you are?
No, instead you run
here and there
helping everyone
but yourself, but
remember, fire goes out
if left unattended.

Taking care of one's self
is not selfish. It is
honoring what God has made.

Child of Now

I am a child of the moment
no yesterday of regrets
or tomorrow's unfulfilled promise.

Only in this moment
do I exist
and for me
that is enough.

Coming Back

Life is a boom-a-rang
bringing back what
we send out.
All my traps
catch mostly me
lies become my shackles.
You'd think I'd learn
but like you
I try it once again.

Toss out good, you say?
Why didn't I think of that?
Think I'll give it a try
some day, but first one more
toss of greed.

Shy

S he runs away and hides
H is adoration she wants
Y et she is too shy

The Bag

We try to fill
a bag with
a hole in the bottom
leaving a trail
of disappointment.
Nothing we grab
fills the bag
leaving us wanting
once again
all the while
complaining that
God's unfair.

Gratitude #5

Today I am grateful
for my sense of smell
delicious bread baking
lilacs in the spring
fragrances on the wind
fill me with gratitude
once again.

Something for Nothing

We want the gold
but don't want to
work the mine.
We tell the government
"give me" and complain
about taxes.
We're jealous when
our neighbors have more.

Something doesn't
come from nothing.
Put the rabbit
in the hat
before you do your trick.

Cartoon Illusion

My calendar
is like a hand-made
cartoon book that
shows characters
move as you quickly
flip through the pages.
Faster and faster
I run creating
the illusion
that I'm going somewhere.

Golden Baskets

She sits weaving
golden grass into
baskets famous
for miles around
each with a flourish
of unique design.
Each blade she
turns, bends, and twists
to catch the light
in its golden shine.

She does not know
what each basket
will carry, he who
buys the basket
will decide how
it will be filled.

Her job is to make
the basket of golden grass
with love and care and
this she does each time.

How like these baskets
are we. God makes
each unique then
it is we who must
decide what goes
in our own:
the glitter o love
or dark mounds
of prejudice and greed.

Gratitude #6

Flowers in the meadow
rainbow in the sky
birds singing in treetops
how blessed are you and I.

Today I am grateful to be
part of this beautiful Earth.
I will do my part to protect
all God has so generously made.

My Bubble

I blew a bubble
it followed me
globe of iridescent colors
became my best friend.

My bubble and I
go everywhere
never is it left behind
for it is my constant
companion until
the end of time.

I call my pretty bubble
God and pray to it each day.
People laugh and say
its an illusion
God can't be a bubble
you fool
but I just smile
and walk away.

Train to Where?

    I'm riding a train
    to nowhere
    faster and faster it goes
    I hope I get there soon
    but to where nobody knows.

Already Been

    I'm going where
    I've already been
    it seems to keep happening
    again and again.
    You'd think I'd learn
    but I don't
    my mistakes have become
    my friends.

Who Is Wealthy?

You are not wealthy
until you give
your wealth away.
The pauper is richer
than the miserly king.
Build your castle within
fill it with God's Light
then give it all away
to know what it feels
like to be truly wealthy.

Once a Bully

Bullies in the playground
grow up to be leaders
in the land
why people vote for them
I never will understand.

Spring Ecstasy

Springtime ecstasy
explosion of flowers
sweet morning air
new babies in the woods
and pasture
joyous life everywhere.

I fall in love with life
every spring. It's so good
to be outdoors
seeing spiders making webs
with strings of dewdrops
my love of all God's creation
goes on forever more.

Pretty?

"Pretty is as pretty does"
my grandmother used to say.
She was right, you know.
Give me the beauty of
a loving person
over a cold hearted
beauty queen any day.

Lord, help me to
say and do love-filled
words and actions
to all I meet
along the way.

Soul Silence

The soul lives
in the silence between breaths.
It needs no reason for being
it just is.

One by one I'm letting go
of projects and activities
that use to fill my day too full
learning how to be
in this life without
justification
to learn who I am
and where I fit
in God's plan.

Gratitude #7

Today I am grateful
for laughter, smiles
and giggles, eyes that twinkle
belly laughs shared
with friends and family
and all whom I meet
along the way.

Life Revealed

I stopped asking questions
letting life reveal itself
or remain a mystery.

No more searching
for answers
the quest has ended.
Life is what it is
that's all I need to know.

What's Within

      The sculptor sees
  the image within the rock
      not just its ridges
     and crevices outside.
     Diamonds are hidden
      inside the heart
   of he who knows how
    to bring them forth.

     Look for treasure
    within all for it is
  there that beauty begins.

Gift of Insomnia

    Insomnia becomes
  a gift when the time
    is used to listen
to what God was waiting
  to tell us and we were
    too busy to hear.

Promises

    Promises

soon forgotten
in politics and love
underlying intention
is seldom clear

Transparent Man

The transparent man
comes in a box
all of his parts
you can see
except for one
the manufacturer left out
his soul that lives through eternity

Cycles

Water boils
becomes steam
joins the clouds
rains on the other
side of the world
becomes a river
that goes to the sea
which someday
returns to me

Life cycles are all around us
seeds to trees which
eventually become
compost for new life

in the floresta

Even I will join this
circle of life so when
it is my time to go
bury me deep and
plant a tree where
I lie that new life
can spring
into eternity

Think Again

How is it that calm, rational behavior
seems insane? Confusion, fear
profound greed are the norm.

Sit and think positive thoughts
you say, we create our own reality.
Is this true? My thoughts created
this world gone mad?
If so, please give me a lobotomy.

No, instead I'm going to end
this "New Age" quest
the spiritual competition
has become absurd.
While I'm at it
I'll give up
religion, rituals, and ohms.
Go for a walk in the floresta instead.

The Patience of God

How patient You are
accepting my fickle love
my doubts and fears
counterfeit promises
I seldom fulfill.

How great is Your love
that space of resurrection
sacred love within love.

Your listening silence
surrounds me, patiently waiting
for me to stop pretending.

I want to love You
truly I do
but first I must search
for I have not yet learned
that what I yearn for
is You.

Someday, when these
words turn to tears
perhaps I will be ready
to accept, even cherish
Your love
'til then what shall I do?

No Secrets

Love cannot be kept
a secret
it's shown in

so many ways.
It refuses to stay hidden
popping out here and there.

Can you not see
the twinkle in my eyes
when you appear
the smile that
brushes my lips?

You are my Beloved
I, your willing slave
bewildered from knowing
that you love me, too.

Let's throw caution
to the wind
put our love
in the open.
We were the only ones
who didn't know
we were lovers anyway.

Cloak of Helplessness

My neck
as thin as a spindle
cannot support my
head, which topples off
and rolls across the floor.

I give away all I own
throw caution to the wind
wander everywhere

going nowhere
to so many places
I've already been.

Helplessness I wear
like a cloak
before my search
even begins.

I don't know what
I'm looking for
nor that I've had it
all the time.

Counting Leaves

I peer into the faces
of strangers
looking for you.

I count leaves
Falling, making piles
of yellow, orange, red.
It doesn't help at all.

Wood smoke goes up
the chimney carrying
my heart with it, too.
I float across the glen
hoping to find you
holding this smoke
filled heart of mine.
I am absurd
I know this, of course

but love has made me a fool.
To me, life is not worth living
unless it is lived with you.

Monk's Wine

The monk's wine of Tuscany
is known throughout the land.
Father Hic-up checks its quality
there's always a glass in his hand.

He toasts each prayer
on the rosary
with humble heart
and bent knees.

His work is not hard
at all. Wine taster
lay down before you fall.

Gratitude #8

Today I am grateful
for sleep. That sweet
time when I lay my
burden's down
snuggle in a cozy bed
and trust the angels
to watch over me.

A Rambling Fool

Am I drunk?
I can't remember
so perhaps I'm sober.

Why am I here?
No, not on this corner
but here on Earth?
What is my purpose
my destination?
I have no idea.

Who speaks these words
looks out of my eyes
listens with my ears?
A rambling fool
who watches ribbons
of morning light
and heads home
though I know
not where.

One By One

Quietly I sit
pen in hand
waiting
drip, drip, drip
the words come
one by one.

I do not think them
I expect they are
stored in the ink
of my pen.

Or perhaps they
really do come from
Source
but who or what
Source is
I do not know.
Nor do I know
where he/she/it
is, if not in
the ink of this pen.

Is there a Source
of creativity
from which we
draw ideas, music, art?

I do not know
I just know
I'm called each morning
to sit quietly and wait
for the words to come
one by one.

Vision Without Eyes

I had a vision
that I could see
even though I was blind.

'Twas late at night
my eyes were closed
yet every detail
of this room I could see.

The door of the prison
opens wide when one's
heart is open, too.

I am who I am
in an old woman's body
in spirit a young
damsel am I
for the spirit does not
sag or wrinkle
always fresh
as morning dew.

I flow out
in an ever widening
spiral, past the stars
and into the arms
of eternity.

Everywhere

The One I love
is everywhere
how can I possibly
love all of God?
My head is in a frenzy
my love spread too thin.

Be at peace, Dear One
I hear Him say
Love with your heart
for there love has no limit.
It grows, fills
overflows even into
the Great Beyond.

All Children

We are all children
playing at life
the only grown-ups
are those free of desire.
The rest of us
are filled with lust and greed
riding make-believe ponies
made with mother's broom.

Knowledge Is Not Wisdom

We are like
a donkey loaded with books
lots of knowledge
but not a bit of wisdom.

Spirituality can not
be learned
it is only experienced.
Can you hear a symphony
by reading the score?

Fool's Play

There is nothing ordinary
each snow flake, leaf, star
is unique, beautifully designed
by our Creator.

The same is true of people
created in all shapes, sizes, color.
Do you hate one leaf on a tree
and love another?
Is one grain of sand
more deserving
than the other?

Do you love one star
and try to extinguish
its neighbor?
There is only
one kingdom
one King,
all else is fool's play.

The Perfect Pear

Perfect pear so sweet
Golden, delicious, am I
Pear shape, at last, is in

The Beggar and Dog

>Beggar on the street
>loves his dog when no one
>can love him anymore

War

>War is not glorious
>there are no heroes.
>There is only the insanity
>of killing for greed and power.
>
>Body parts lie scattered
>on fields of death
>hands that will never again caress
>feet that can no longer walk in fields of corn
>faces twisted in eternal agony
>stench of fresh blood, bowels emptied.
>
>I do not want to hear songs
>which tell the glory and honor of war.
>Give me my husband next to me
>on a cold winter night.
>Let him swing his daughter high in the air
>and hear her squeals of delight.
>His mother's sorrow matches my own
>as we see his chair forever empty
>at our table laden with his favorite food.
>
>Be gone with men marching
>to the cadence of drums beating
>flags flapping, voices chanting
>lies of war.

A baby lies silent along side
her mother, dog, grandmother
shattered like the walls of their home
blasted by errant bombs
and uncaring men.

I will not even write of women
who participate in war
denying their life-giving essence.
How can you participate in taking lives,
when you are created to give life?

No, you will never convince me
that bombing schools, homes, hope
leads to peace.

Democracy, you shout
freedom!
Can we be free with
blood on our hands
and men returned
with shattered lives?

Let the billions of dollars
Spent on war clean up the slaughter
of generations of greed.
Shout, "No more!" loud and clear.
Pray that never again will a bomb
blast a family's dreams and hope
for peace on Earth.

Let the bells toll in a new year
that heralds the end of wars
and the beginning of an earth
of untold beauty, love and Oneness.
This is my prayer, my dream, my cry.
Join my voice and sing of love

in a world that honors life.

My Piece of Land

I stand on land
which I claim
as my own
deed in my hand
I survey my domain.

Space of love
carefully created
planted with fruits
vegetables, and flowers galore.
Clusters of bananas
hang with immense purple flowers
pineapples stand in star-burst rows.
Monkeys swing from bamboo
to trees filled with guavas
sweet and vermilion within.

I've planted trees for shade
each one chosen for its
flowering beauty and regal stance.
There are hammocks and benches
inviting us to rest beneath
whispering boughs
stream wanders past
wearing a necklace of
colorful impatients
tiny flowers that remind
us to not be in a hurry.

A crane steps carefully
to sip the clear, cool water

born of a spring nearby.

I sigh with contentment
at my home in the floresta
and know this piece of paper
is not true. For we never
own the land, but rather
are caretakers for the Divine
we must love this space
and leave it better
than when we came.

The Impossible

If you made a list
of all of the things
you say are impossible
filled page after page
let your imagination run wild
you would still fail
to capture it all.

Libraries are full of books
with tales of fantasy
science fiction and make believe
that we are certain could never be.

But what if each creature
place and idea actually exist
in dimensions and locations
we have not yet explored?

What if these wild fantasies of our minds
are ancient memories stored

in our genes and passed down
to awaken in time?

Open your mind
to unlimited possibilities
you are still thinking
quite small
for worlds exist
for us to know
when we have the courage
to step into our fantasies
and become One with All.

Science and Mysticism

I've moved from petri dishes
to mystical visions.
"Prove it to me"
changed to astral travel
scientific certainty
became quantum guessing.

But then, I never thought God
belonged in a beaker
or that love can be proved
with complicated formulas.

Let me rock a baby
watch a foal being born at sunrise
and I will trade all the limiting
scientific theories
for the delight
of dancing in dew wet grass
on a full moon night with

star light shimmering in my hair.

The Candle

There sits on the table
a candle, you say
light is what I see.
I do not seek to change your vision
nor should you wish to change mine.

My light sits on top of
your candle, each in its
own reality. Can one exist
without the other?
Let us wait and see.

Helping

Helping hurts others
When it steals the chance to learn
Check your motives first

A Moment in Time

Today I lie on sun-warmed clouds
Gentle breezes caress me
soothing a false sense of urgency.
This tiny moment in time
mere blink, a sigh, fills me

with the certainty of my
existence within my Creator.
We are One.

In Its Time

All comes in its time
walk in serenity knowing
that each moment evolves
changing the kaleidoscope
patterns of life.

Go slowly, no need to rush
what you do not do today
is not today's work.
Surrender to what you
cannot control
which are most things, you know.

Life is much simpler
than you make it.
Learn from nature–
cycles unfolding with
slow motion grace.

Become a gently moving
upward spiral.

Patterns in Nature

Pay attention to patterns

all around, nature's
designs of star bursts
spirals, heart shapes
circles, triangles
leaves unfurling with care
Fibonacci codes: 3, 5, 7, 11
abound in petals, leaves
branching of rivers, lightening
even our veins.

The world was made with
meticulous care, each part
dove-tailed with master craft.
Then came man who relentlessly
consumes and destroys
pollutes, cuts, mines
ignoring nature's laws
without remorse.

The time of reckoning
is upon us, our Mother
screams her agony
around the globe.
Thousands of souls
are leaving, animals
disappear into extinction.
How much must man
suffer before he wakes up
and sees his greed
will be his demise?

Following this tidal wave
of destruction, is a
force of hope
building across the Earth.
Light workers armed with
healing love lead the

awakening of millions
calling for people to step
forward and claim their souls.

The scale tips back and forth
precariously, balance no
guarantee. But each of
us working to restore
the intricate patterns
of life our Creator gave us
can make a difference
that will last through eternity.

Absolute Truths

No longer do I believe in
the stability of truth.
Mercurial, vaporous truths
changing with time, cultures,
expediency, points of view.

What was absolute truth
for me before is no more
became dust the wind blew away.
At first, this frightened me
the false security of my
blinders ripped from my eyes.
I was dazzled by thoughts
and memories, floods of
possibilities left me in awe.

Piece by piece the puzzle
is being revealed once
we are willing to consider

that all that we were taught
was designed to imprison
our thoughts, to hide
our power to create with
our minds, to walk in
multiple dimensions.

We are creators
with our Creator.
All starts with a thought
a "what if" gives birth to all.

Walk away from distractions
that dull your ability
to think, to create, to be.

The Silent Breath

We mark our time
with silent breaths
in and out, in and out.
My soul rides each breath
as I merge with the Divine.

Yard Sale Junk

Yesterday's dreams and hopes,
memories of shared love,
lie heaped on a table
with a sign
"Reduced for Quick Sale."

My mother's favorite pot
nightgown never used
saved for just the right
occasion which never came
pictures of people we no longer
remember, mixed with those
of us as kids, memories none
of us want anymore
carelessly tossed away.

One day my mother's house
was filled with her life's treasures
next day a neighbor asks
Is this junk for sale, too?

What if?

What if man
instead of seeking to destroy each other
rose to a level of love and compassion
where he saw the perfection of light and dark?
In this place exists both, and
he would work in love and peace
to transmute the dark energy
to the higher vibrations
of love and light.

In this space of love
would exist a doorway of healing
for dark energies to come
to be transmuted.

Can I love to this degree?

Fill my eyes with compassion
Let me cry, "They know not what they do!"
May I be so free of judgement
that there is never a reason to forgive.

Can I see cycles of horror
not as endless evil
but rather as evolving spirals
moving ever upward into the light?

Power

Power, dominion, enslavement
So you want power, do you?
No problem! I can give you
more than you can ever imagine.
All will be yours to command
as you please.

Countries around the world
will jump at the chance to
do as you command; beautiful women
will call you to their beds.
What else do you dream of: mansions
yachts, travel, the finest wines
money, gold, jewels...all will be yours!

Power, sweet power, now it
is mine. Let the fools make
peace signs with their fingers
wear flowers in their hair.
Throw the dogs a bone
I laugh as I watch them
fight for that morsel

their hunger and desperation
to live making them savage.

Power is a snake in your hand.
You brandish it like a sword
stabbing here and there.
The snake's deadly bite
brings death to those
who dare to oppose you.

Beware that the snake
does not turn on the hand
that holds it, it's poison
mixing with your own.

The power of the Dark
is built with illusion, lies, and deceit.
It cannot stand against the Light.
Note how Mother Earth
in a breath's instance
washed match box cities
into the ocean
her belly splits open
pouring fire and wrath
on all; in a blink, thousands die.
Our Mother Earth has power, indeed.

Know that the Source
of her power is greater
than your mind can conceive.
The Dark is nothing, a brat
strutting, full of foul air.

Source waits and watches
as we play our foolish games,
destroying our world and ourselves
with our greed and lust for power.

There is a time of reckoning
for each of us, our deeds do not go
unnoticed; think carefully before
you choose whom you serve.

Humility, gratitude, and love
bring you into the
family of light, banishing
darkness from your soul.
Which do you choose?

Our Family

All are our family
Everyone's God's creation
There are no borders

Wake-Up Call

Heroes are often made
during great tragedies.
The horror of death
and destruction making
us reach inside for that
which is pure and strong
extending our hands
in love to friends and enemies alike.

Wake-up, brothers and sisters
find your hearts within

know who you are
and what you can be.

One Tiny Flower

Out of the rubble of twisted cars
mountains of fallen buildings
ashes of fire uncontrolled
grows a tiny flower
reaching its face to the sun.

It is God's promise of life
all is not lost
tomorrow is yet to come.

Our Defects

See your defects
as gifts to help you grow.
Thank God for your sorrow
your tragedies, your sins
for each bring you closer
to the Divine.

Next, when you see a defect
in another, thank God
for giving this person a
gift as good as yours.

Love Beacon

How can I learn to
love so completely
that I become a beacon
pulsating to the world
this transforming
energy of God?

Take away all that
causes me to falter:
fear, pride, lost hope
fill me to overflowing
sending out love's healing light.

Mathematics of Love

One + one = two
That cannot be true!
1 + 1 = 1
When All is One!

Courage

Men faint from needles
women run and scream from mice.
But when the need is real
heroes are born
reaching out to help
across oceans of differences
united by compassion.

Puzzle of Life

When we open our minds
to explore ideas we thought
impossible before, we
attract sources of
knowledge of all kinds.

Do not judge is it "good" or "bad,"
but consider each a piece
of the puzzle of life
that we need to add
to the wisdom that we gain.

All experiences we have
are but lessons to learn
from a position of acceptance
and love.
The door has opened
step out of the box
which you thought was safe
but now has become a cage.
You can operate with a
frequency of fear
or that of love–
only you can decide
which to choose.

Reality Mirrors Itself

What is my reality of the world?
Do I view people as untrustworthy
and self-centered? Is life hard
too much work, not enough
money? Am I disappointed
with my life?

What does it mean
that we create our
own reality? Do we
cause disasters and death
with our pessimism
and discontentment?
What does it mean
"reality mirrors itself?"

Today, I woke up happy,
no, more than happy–grateful
looking forward to
another day.
I now know how precious
life is, regardless of
how events unfold.
No matter what happens today
when I go to bed tonight
I will be happy–no more, than happy.
I will be grateful for this day
will you?

Manifesting Life #1

Be aware of your fears

they block the
vibration of love.
When you feel that
cold hand clutch you
call the fear by its name.
Take slow, deep breaths
call for the Light.
As it fills you, see it
wash away the fear.
You are a powerful
channel of Source.

Your Mission

Being here on Earth
is not happen stance.
Life is not random at all.
Look at the concise design
of all that is, created
with minute detail.

How do you fit into
God's scheme of life?
You are not a grain of sand, nor
a drop of rain in the ocean.
You are a Being of Light,
powerfully filled with the Divine.

Your mission can not be done
by anyone else.
Step forward to claim it now.

Manifesting Life #2

When we observe animals, we see
they have past knowledge.
Our genes and DNA carry ancient
wisdom we need today.
State your intention to go
within and tap this reserve.
Visualize and follow the infinity
symbol over your Third Eye.
Trace its spiral into your past
know who you are.

Lotus

Consider the possibility
that we exist in multiple
forms and dimensions
at the same time
universes within universes
human on earth
lizard in star nation,
plant on another planet
celestial being guarding others
member of the Family of Dark.

There are many unanswered
questions. Perhaps some
lie in worlds of possibilities.
Open your mind to perceive
your existence as a
lotus flower–beautiful
layers of petals.

Your Secret Sin

Most of us have a secret sin
we hope no one ever knows.
Tiny or large, it eats away
our self-respect, leaving
us embarrassed at its memory
ashamed that we failed
did something we knew
was wrong.

To heal this blight on our soul
we must do three things:
make restitution if we can
asking forgiveness for whom
we have harmed
humbly ask God's pardon
and finally, forgive ourselves
vowing never to fail in this again.

Accept this forgiveness, get rid
of this pain. Tell someone you trust
what you have done
for a burden shared is less heavy.
Sometimes forgiving ourselves
is the hardest part,
but hanging onto guilt
can become the sin of pride.

You are Beloved, your soul
is Divine. Learn the lesson, then
let it go; be at peace and walk in love.
You are One with the Creator.

That Man

I don't like that man
he is unlovable to me.
See how he acts!
His way is not mine
like him I could never be.

I love God with
all of my heart.
I do good deeds
when I can.
But I do wonder why
God made such a man
so imperfect that
I cannot love him
then made such
a good man as me.

The Takers

Takers are those
so consumed by their desires
that they ruthlessly
take from others without
a thought of their harm.
Countries stand raped of
all that can be sold
their people oppressed
and left with naught.

Takers climb corporate ladders
on the backs of others
do not see the neighbor's
widow and children needing
a helping hand, their own
family's needs often ignored.
Money, power, addictions drive
the taker. His ruthless greed
cataracts on his eyes of love.

Being a taker or a giver
is one of life's choices
basic, yet profound.
Which do you choose to be?

Manifesting Life #3

Beware of hypocrisy; get rid of
malicious behavior and deceit.
Be done with jealously, backstabbing
arrogance, pettiness and greed.
Don't just pretend your goodness
all puffed up and proud.
Crave the pure spiritual milk of
humility, honor and love.
Cry out for this nourishment, to
become all you can be.

Prophecy #3 – Time Jumpers

How stable is time?

Many time zones exist
We sleep while another is awake
One day behind, another ahead.

Is time only a construe of our minds
or is it frequency based?
Can we expand our consciousness
into other time periods
time jumpers, explorers, treasure hunters
adjusting their vibrational levels to move
backward and forward in time?

Many have already arrived
to share in this momentous event
more are coming. What is the
treasure they seek?

Be aware of your value
know that your very thoughts
are seeds the future. You are
a creator building with
the frequency of love.
We are raising the frequency from
one of fear and hate
to the ecstasy of creating
with the Divine.

The time is now.

Me?

One by one they fall away
people, desires, dreams, fears
masks, games–stripped and gone.

What will be left when
outer wrappings and distractions
are no more? What is the
inner most core of who I am?
Not a mother, father, sister
brother, friend, or enemy...
just this inner light of me.
I am who I am
But who and what am I?

4x4's

Happy to be sad
Hungry to be full
Peaceful in my anger
Shy in my boldness

Doubts when I'm certain
Insanity mixed with clarity
Abhor what I love
Life is a paradox

Hope

Hope
Our Strength
Keeping us afloat
Dreams filled with promises
Hope and faith go together.

Faith and Hope

I hope my husband
remembers to bring milk.
He has never forgotten
anything I asked him to bring.
I have faith that he'll bring milk.

Why isn't it that simple
with God? I ask for
something and hope
I'll get it. If I don't
I am disappointed.
God didn't answer my prayer.

God is not a vending machine!.
If I didn't get what I
asked for, maybe the answer was
"No!" or perhaps, "Not yet"
or even, "You are not ready for that."

Why don't I have as much
faith in God as I do in my husband?

Sin

Sin, a guilt-producing word
thoughts are sinful, too
there's no escape
Now what?
Love.

Prophecy #4 – Balance

A fine line has always existed
between genius and insanity
good and evil, dark and light
all are two sides of the coin.

A fine balance is what you seek
that space where you know each well.
It is then that we can maintain
the frequencies of balance
knowing as our Creator knows
even as a parent knows, that their
children will grow up and be fine.

Let's put aside our martyrdom, our fear
replace it with a playful respect for
our foible's, with no offense to others.
Let's play and have fun with this
Renaissance so profound as to be
recorded in the annals of time.

Our Angry Mother

Mother Earth is angry
filled with vengeance and wrath.
She is slow to anger
but her power is great.
She never lets the guilty go
unpunished; we all share her displeasure.
Whirlwinds, pounding waves that
droughts and fire; who can
stand before her fury?

Mother Nature can be sweet
sprinkling diamond dew drops
on blades of grass, sighing
gentle breezes, scattering
flowers at our feet.

How long will we slash her trees,
pour our slop into her waters
dump tons of toxic chemicals
onto the earth, spread nuclear
destruction across the world
allow the Family of Darkness
to reign supreme?

The time of reckoning is at hand.
Listen to the thunder of her warning
awaken and work with the Light
to bring all back to balance again.

How Precious Your Love

How precious is Your love
I wake up to find You near.
Your presence surrounds me
Your scent is in the air.

I rest in Your arms
eat golden honey from Your hand
sing my love for You, weep tears
of joy at Your blessings, knowing
we walk hand in hand.

Grace

We receive through grace
Unmerited gift of God
Accept – be grateful.

Compliments

The bitter taste of a false compliment
lingers long on the tongue of the giver
and harsh on the ear of the receiver.
Do not seek to ingratiate yourselves with
words you do not mean. Better to be
silent than to paint your pretty words
of falseness and break the trust
of those who know your words
are not sincere.

The Bugle

The bugle sounds to start the day
and plays TAPS to begin the night.
We announce our intentions
on New Year's Day to start anew.
Soon forgotten are these promises
another year slips by
wasted dreams, broken vows
of things we meant to do.

Intention is the key of creation.

Our thoughts become our realities.
Give careful design of your
intention, state it clearly with
firm resolve. Then throughout the day
do what you can to more
that intention to your reality.

All creation begins with a thought
followed by a clear intention
a commitment that, when not broken
becomes a reality.
We are creators with our Creator.
Sound the bugle of a new day
where all humanity knows
who they are and creates together
a world of unparalleled beauty and peace.

The Axe

The mighty axe swings
muscles across the back
ripple as the axe finds its mark.
A rhythm develops, swing-chop
swing-chop, soon the ancient tree
falls shaking the earth and
shouting its dying cry.

The man lovingly cuts wood
for his family to be safe and
give thanks for the fallen tree.
In its place, he plants two
saplings he's raised
to give back to the forest
more than he took

a wise lesson for us all.
He whispers his gratitude
for all nature that gives
to him, both working
in perfect harmony.

Your Words, My Pen

Poet Supreme, put Your words
in my heart, my mind, my pen.
Thousands around the world
are awakening to Your voice.
May we reach out our hands
to form a chain of Love.
Fill us with Your Light
that we may pass it to
those still in darkness.
Help us to remember
who we are–creators
of the One Creator
Beings of Light walking
the Path of Love.

Golden Wheat

Fields of golden wheat
breezes bending, sun sparkling
bread of life for us all.
One tiny grain seems too small
to feed the world, but combined
with others can fill bellies

and hearts around the globe.

Crooked Road

Where are you going
little road that twists
turns back on itself, then
shoots forward with glee?
Over mountains, past well-tended farms
meandering by trout-filled brook
avoiding cities, dark and dirty
the crooked road explores it all.

What do you seek, my onward trail?
What is your destiny?
But the road does not know
where it goes, or where it
wants to be.
How often we live our lives
this way, without plan or thought
just merrily going along
hoping we get there
wherever "there" may be.

Cock's Crow

Cock crows announce the dawn
sliver of moon, confetti of stars
a stillness of anticipation
like lovers who pause before a kiss.
What will this day bring?

Each day of life a precious gift.
One by one they come, then fade away.
Will I be happy today, sad, angry
hungry, full, tired, filled
with boundless energy?

A spectrum of feelings will
color my day, creating a rainbow
of vibrancy, rich and complete.
Would I live without even one?

Sadness shows me how much I care
anger tells me, this I cannot accept.
Hunger makes the simplest food a feast.
Jealously helps me see my fear
that no one will love me.
Fear brings me to the Divine.
Most important is Love, which
balances them all, heals, and
shows me all is one.

The rooster crows again and
I give thanks for whatever
the day may bring knowing
even a bad day is good
when one walks in
gratitude and love.

Rocking Chair

How many miles did she rock each day?
My grandmother's chair never stopped.
Shelling peas, laughing chats

with neighbors who stopped by
and sat with a pan of peas in their laps.
There were miles to be rocked,
life to be lived, my Grandmother was loved by all.

My sister and I played jacks
nearby and listened to stories
we should not have heard.
Flashing knowing smiles, the women
talked in code that we had
learned long ago, but pretended
to not know. We giggled
with delight at those secret tales
of peccadilloes of cousins, uncles, and aunts.
No one escaped a role in these
stories, even our mom and dad.

Sweet memories are created
by the squeak of a loose
board beneath Grandmother's chair
rocking across the lives of us all.

Manifesting Life #4

The fear you meet on
your path is your dark.
The purpose of our lives is
to seek and grow.

The collective global fear
is being in charge of oneself.
We give away our power of
decision-making to others.

Step beyond your fear, and
take back your power today.

God Thinks of Everything

Why do you worry
about everything big and small
filling your mind with "what ifs"
that never come, fears made of smoke?

God made this world with
incredible attention to detail
balance, beauty and design.
Do you think that since He
made you, He would not
give you and your life that
same loving care? Be
at peace knowing that
God thinks of everything.
Trust that all will come out
as it should.

Endurance

Endurance a must
When you fail, just try again
Each success a step

Loving Words

Words
Abusive, foul
Wound the soul
Others and ourselves, too
Speak only loving, honest words

Absolution

Forgive
Merciful, gentle
Enlightening, freeing, healing
Forgive each transgression 70x7
Absolution

False Teachers

We go from one guru to another
Book shelves laden with enlightenment.
We sample religions like candy.
Beware of your heroes, your masters
do not become their slave.

Reciprocal

If I could be completely silent
perhaps this heart of mine could heal
but alas, I am a poet
words bleed from every pore.

Sonnets, rhythms, complete
verses of nonsense
without pause.
The longing in my soul
fertilizes my pen
making silence impossible.

Why do I suffer so?
I expect it's because
I think my love is not
reciprocated.

I stay hungry
in the middle of a feast
too blind to see
what's in front of me.
I long for what
I've always had.

Flame of Light

I am but a candle
burning down until
I am but a flame of light
then a spark
transmuted into
eternal love
of He who made all.

Joyously Sad

When I am apart
from you, I do not exist
even the moon is make believe.
I'm always looking for You
not seeing that You are
always here
seeking endlessly
not knowing
I've already found.
I cry and my tears
become words
calling out to You
Soon crying becomes
my religion
I worship all the time.
I reach to others
and they begin to cry, too
joyously sad that they
have joined the
not-being.

Beggar's Bowl

In the mirror
is my reflection
my shadow is not me.

I'm not the thorn
on the rose either
not the wave or the sea.

If I separated myself

from You, I would not exist
an empty beggar's bowl
is all that I would be.

Call of the Siren

In a boat by myself
no land do I see
I try to stay above
the surface3
but the siren
calls to me.

Shall I take the plunge
find she who calls
from the bottom
of eternity
a fool's decision
who cannot even
decide if he is looking
at sunset or sunrise
on the edge of the sea.

Drunk With Love

I am melting snow.
There's a moon inside of my house.
I run outside looking everywhere.
Have you seen the moon?
I cry, looking up in the sky.

They shake their heads
and walk away
leaving he who is drunk with love
in the garden looking
for what his house
already holds.

The Rock of God

See that stone
that's God lying there
yonder tree, that's God, too.
Even your look is God.
My tongue which spouts
truth but which you think
are the ramblings of a madman
yes, even my tongue and words
are God.
Be quiet, you fool, or they'll
lock you up and throw
away the key.
Doesn't matter if they
lock me up for
God is everywhere
even in you and me.

Silent Poem

I want to write
a poem with no words
and in that silence
you will hear God speak.

Longing

Longing
such an inadequate word
to explain why I go mad
and disappear chasing a moon
which refuses to
stay in the sky
disappearing each month
I know not where.
Longing
my love for You
leaves me invisible
a fragile vial
transparent
filled with need.
Longing
making me
a silent echo
waiting to return
and tell its sad story
one more time.

Consumed

Soon I will fill books
of poetry with only blank pages
for words have become inadequate.
I am slowly disappearing
already my shadow is gone.
Soon there will be an empty space
wherever I stand
a perfect place to plant a tree.
My love for You
has consumed me.
In turn, Your love
for me had captured
my soul which wants
nothing more than to be
with You through eternity.

Endless Words

When will I run out of words?
How many poems are enough
to tell of my love for You?
I've become consumed
with love-madness.
It's not my fault I rave
and fill books with poetry
for what else can I do
with this passion
that only You can satisfy?

Maybe I'll learn another
language or two so I'll
have more words.
I think I've used this one up.
My friends beg me to be quiet
strangers run away
but even my silence
is but a prayer to You.

Only a Shadow

I am but a shadow
of Your love
a single twinkle
from a star
the fragrance of
warm bread
not even a crumb.
You are everything
all things
even this insignificant
poet of useless words.
Never-the-less, I love You
praise You until my friends
ask me to please shut-up.
I'm doing the best I can
though, of course
it's not nearly enough.

Razor's Edge

A spoken sentence
sharpened to a fine edge
cuts as surely
as a barber's razor.
Guard your words, Sir
that they cast not even
a shadow of harm.
Words cannot be retrieved
like marble tossed
on the ground.
Sharp words wound
hearts that bear their
marks indefinitely.
If you cannot control
this viper tongue
then open not your mouth
for silence is the only cure
for he whose words
know not compassion.

The Lottery

He stands in line
to buy tickets of hope
murmuring prayers
to the lottery god
thinking rich
is synonymous with happy.
Every week he visits
this house of fools
with all the others
who think being
a winner guarantees
serenity.

Madly Serene

I am calm
even serene
others think
I've gone mad
walking around smiling
petting puppies
playing checkers in the park
with a homeless old man
sniffing rainbows
only I can see
Mad? Perhaps
but please don't cure me
for I finally
belong to myself.

My Pen Knows

Does my pen know
what it's writing?
Endless words
packed inside
waiting for paper
to release its blather.
Thank goodness mules don't talk.
Not even for a half-a-breath
do I know who I am
a shadow walking in circles
has more sense than me.

Writing endlessly
my words become
silent
for after all
a fool in love
has nothing
worth saying.

Hollow

I feel empty, hollow
separated from Source
like a silent flute
with no air
no sounds come out
silent in my longing.
Any lover apart from
his beloved, knows
what I'm saying.
You can't see silence
nor hear its message
so I suffer alone
my flute empty
of all music
bewildered
seeking solace
in a wine
with no taste
tears that fill my heart
but refuse to fall from my eyes.
Mine is a fine love
full of surrender.
My life filled with
days of wanting
longing, an empty note
from a silent flute.

The Thirsty Fish

I am but a thirsty fish
who drinks the ocean dry
then has no place to swim.
I eat the seeds of the papaya
thinking I can grow
a forest inside and
never again be hungry.
Don't call me foolish
though I know it's true.
I can't get enough
of my Beloved.
Please be compassionate
with me for I am in love
and walk a crooked
line like a drunk
overflowing with wine
content to be helplessly
intoxicated having no need
for respectability.

Become the Sky

I am going to slide
out of the side of the cloud
and become the sky.

Filling universes upon universes
I make my escape
into the Great Beyond
where there is only
light and love
into which I merge
and become
One with All.

Empty

We rush to fill
the emptiness
buy a new car
take a new lover
frantically we
stuff that
hole of the soul.
What does this silence
within represent
loneliness
abandonment
no, it is your
salvation
once you know how
to sit in silence
erase your name
and release your soul
into the Divine.

Bound By Fear

Our fears keep us bound
terrified of change.

We gobble down stories
of what might come
gorge on what-ifs
until we burst
in this gluttony of fear.

Stop listening to these whispers
they are your worst enemy
yet you cling to them
terrified to
simply let go.

Tree of Respect

Grow a tree of respect
if respect is what you
want to harvest.
Apples do not grow
on a lemon tree.

Plant a money tree
in your back yard
but remember that
you can't make a pie
from its fruit.

Want and need
are two different things.
Learn to distinguish
between the two.

Contentment
is not a product
of more
but rather

comes with
surrender.

God?

For those who
don't believe in God
life must seem very hard
a crap shoot
with little luck.
I think there is a
Universal Loving Intelligence
and if I am wrong
I still find comfort
in the idea and choose
this way to live.

P

Pansy, pie, puddle
pat, possibility
people, preacher
poetry
perhaps
pain
peace
probably
persistent
passion
pretty puppies
prayer

The Ballerina

I know a frog
who is a ballerina
impossible you say
legs too long
all that hoppin'
too green, mouth too big
croaks too loud
frogs can't be ballerinas

But the frog doesn't know
twirling, leaping
dancing from lily pad to another
happy to be a ballerina.

Free

How is it that we
act freely but are compelled?
Intellectual questions are useless
only the soul spears the truth.

The mind cannot follow
the soul into illumination
and wonder.
Awe is a gift
use it wisely.

Change

C an expect change in all things
H iding from the inevitable does not work
A llow transformation with an eager heart
N othing escapes change
G o with the flow is good advice
E volution depends on change

The Vessel

Laugh at lightening
ignore the thunder
add tears of joy
to the rain
sleep peacefully
in the consciousness
of God.
We are but an empty vessel
waiting to be filled
with God's love.

Become All

If you are not with God
you are nowhere.
I am not my brother's keeper
I am my brother.
Be empty

seek nothing
that you may become all.

My Enemy?

Come, my enemy
let us sit facing
each other in silence
for in this quiet
our hearts can speak
with patience
compassion
until we find
the silver chord
of love which
connects all beings.

In Love With Love

I'm in love
with love
not my lover.
I love the idea of love
though its reality
often ends up messy.

I have no wings
yet I fly
into other worlds
where only lovers can go.

My spirit needs no food
Love's very scent is
nourishment.
He who loves
knows no hunger.

What It Is

Life is what it is
sometimes up
sometimes down.
We complain
blame
or accept.

Be grateful for the good
make the best of the bad
just doin' the best
we can.

Finding Pearls

I'm finding pearls everywhere
Not just in translucent oyster shells
I1m making a necklace that circles the world
I'm finding pearls everywhere
Each pearl is full of love
It's found by eyes that see only God
I'm finding pearls everywhere
Not just in translucent oyster shells

What Is Life?

How can anyone say
what life is all about?
It is a question with many answers
a question with no answers.

Rosebuds are sweet
shiny green leaves
soft thorns that prick.
Roses in full bloom
casting aromas divine
dotting the garden with
colors regal
leaves full of black spot
thorns hard that rip and stab.

A baby smells sweet
until his diaper is full.
Guess that is what life
is about- sweet baby smells
and a bit of poop!

Weaving Moonbeams

Don't be satisfied to live other people's stories
create your own myth.
Refuse to let circumstances
define who you are.

Find laughter in the wind
Plant a pretty tree
weave moonbeams
on a star-filled night

Be all, be nothing
it's the same

Just Being

Not doing anything these days
it is a hard thing to do
no book, TV, music
tapping of my toes
jiggling of my feet
nothing
leaving my mind open
free of shoulds
it is terrifying
almost impossible
just to be

Sitting in the Sun

I come here every day
and pray the prayer of silence.
This prayer seeks no favor
it is enough to just
sit with the Sun
in gratitude and surrender.

Good Enough

In case you didn't notice
I'm still here
still trying, still hoping

to get it right
and when I don't
to accept that
perfection is a trap
of discontent
and "good enough"
is good

I Am Light

Early I rise
and discover that moment
each day when night dies
and a new morning is born.
All around is the sweet music
of life, a few notes here, there
until the symphony begins

The doe and I silently sip
in the clear stream
then leap and play
chasing each other
in a flower-filled meadow
until time opens
the door to another world
where I merge
into the joy of life
becoming the dew drops
on the grass reflecting
the morning sun.

I am Light
which is what
I was meant to be.

In a Time Before

In a time before
thinking and imagining
did I exist
if so, how, where, why?
In a time before
desire ruled the world
did harmony play
a sweet melody?
Could it be
that there was
no beginning
nor will there be
an end

just a coming
and going
until infinity?

Our Addictions

We love our addictions
forgive their faults
rationalize our downfall
defend our need
not understanding
that the closer we
draw to God
the less we need
of this world.

Dear Lord

take me in your arms
that I will be safe
from all harm.

Follow the Light

Which way do
I turn, where
should I go?
I am lost
in a world
of confusion
and woe.

There is only
one direction, my child
turn neither left or right
move forward with certainty
just follow My Light.

Our Strength

Never brag about being strong
A mere breeze turned wind can take you away
True strength come only for the Lord
Never brag about being strong
Only in surrender do we gain strength
It is our love of God that makes us strong
Never brag about being strong
A mere breeze turned wind can take you away

The Secret of Life

If only life were a belly rub
how happy I would be
I'd howl at the moon
scratch at a flea.
Me and my dog
know the secret to joy
a belly rub
cup of coffee
and our favorite toy.

Just God

There is no reality but God.
This concept stretches my mind.
It has the ring of truth
but how can this be?

That table
the tree from which
it was made
an illusion
or reality?

Are we but thoughts of God?
How crazy He must be
for this world is full
of madness
thoughts turned
to reality.

A Wise One

I need to find a wise person.
Have you seen one today?
I don't want one
who is knowledgeable
as this is a bait
for popularity.
Knowledge has no soul.
Ah, but one who is wise
knows and shares
the way of God.

Live Your Life

I cannot live
your life for you
you must find your own way.
Neither I, Lady Luck
not even God
maps our path
only our own decisions
each day.

Irony of Inspiration

You come here every day
looking for inspiration
to reassure yourself that
life is good
your life has meaning
there is a loving God.

But instead, I tell you
that while I'm glad you're here
all that you seek
you already have.
It's the irony of the year.

Rosebud

Every time I think
I have an original idea
Google search gives
thousands of citations
leaving me humbled
once again
yet a new rose but
sprinkled with morning dew
still delights
though we've seen them
many times before.

Why Kiss?

Why do we kiss?
a moment of connection
an expression of caring
even a final goodbye

K eeping souls joines
I nto the Great Beyond
S oul therapy
S oul transfer

Sugar Cane

The monkeys love sugar cane
quickly stripping away the
tough outside to reach
the sweetness within.

My lover has discovered
the same about me
says he
a bit tough on the outside
but, ah-h-h
the sweetness within.

He's right, of course
my outer toughness
protects the soft sweetness
that others want to steal
to suck dry leaving
a hard core
that cannot
longer bend
in the wind
thus is broken.

Union

My longing for You
pulls me forward
like a wench
this God-love moves
me toward
union with the Divine.

I go eagerly
like a bride to her groom
blushing in anticipation

for only sweet union
will quench this
fire of desire.

World of Fools

Sometimes I forget completely
that You are always near.
Like a fool, I run here and there
asking everyone
where You are.

But I live in a world of fools
who also do not know
You are everywhere.

Like dervishes, we twirl
in the madness
of our need
ignoring the light
while searching
for the Sun.

Rich or Poor?

I am so poor
the beggars run
from me
my clothes so full
of holes the naked
would not want them.

Yet I walk around
with a smile on my face

breaking into song
or laughter
with random joy.

Children laugh
and follow me
weaving like drunks
twirling fingers
by their ears.

But I ignore them all
knowing serenity
rich in the golden
Light of Your love.

Light I Cannot See

I am searching
for illumination
ignoring the candle
in my hand.
I look at the sun
see only dark clouds.
The moonbeams no longer
show me the way.

I am lost in darkness
blind to the light
that spills forth
from a heart full
of longing
and eyes that
cannot see.

The Garden

Do not worry about
that which is transient
live as a butterfly
in a garden
filled with nectar.

Take on sip at a time
trusting the gardener
will keep the flowers
in bloom.

Pit of Madness

I've climbed out
of the pit of madness
leaving behind
ghosts of fear
and dark shadows.

My clothes are tattered
hair all askew
face streaked with dried tears
yet illumination
radiates from within
God's love fills me
leading me home.

Wonder of Love

Hope turns to faith
as God's blessings
fill me with light

and I finally understand
the wonder of love.

Love Endures

Fame is followed
by fall
greed by emptiness
power is an illusion
only love endures.

Complaints

Complaints erode
like the drip of water
boring a hole through
a rock
turn off the faucet.

Flying

I finally realized
I can fly
and take to wing
wonder why I
sat there so long.

Spiritual Arrogance

Do not use the name of God
to control another.

Spiritual arrogance
is a fool's game.

Fear does not breed love
speak not of the fires of hell
eternal damnation
suffering separation
from the Light.

Our God, the only God
is merciful, loving
without condition
or exception.

There is none but He
until beyond eternity.

A Single Drop

Can a single drop
wet the ocean
the flicker of a candle
light the sky?

Yet God knows
each drop in the sea
the names of each star
each flicker they give.

Your love may seem
inconsequential
but it becomes
as the sun
when filled with
God's grace
love without end.

Poppy Promises

White gold of the poppy
casts souls into hell
a few drops of promise
delivers living death
to fool who
run from fear.

Co-creators of Light

Penny for your thoughts
is a poor price indeed
for from our thoughts
come our creativity.

We are co-creators
from the Creator Supreme
bringing Light into
the world shadowed by greed.

Let the Light shine
through you
illuminating your soul
and into the Great Beyond.

Just One Note

A single note
in a symphony
cannot the music make
but combined with the others
lifts all it touches
to the Lord.

Slice of Pie

I'm taking a hunk of pie
a little slice will never do
Grandma's love cut in slices
just one is not enough

Cat's Purr

A cat's purr
sweet contentment
throaty song
singing, "all is well."

Illusions

You sit in prison
not knowing the door
is unlocked.
Confinement is an illusion
you accept
when love could
set you free.

Love or Not

Everything has to do
with loving or not loving
taking, not taking
doing *to* another
or *for* another.
It's all about
loving or not loving.

If you think this
is not true
then you have not looked
deeply enough
for always there's
the choice
to love or not.

What You Want

You do not know
what you want.
You try this and that
nothing satisfies
this yearning
yet your heart knows.

Let yourself be pulled
to that for which
you long, for what
you truly love will
draw you to this desire.

Ocean Music

The ocean is a symphony
silver fish darting here and there
like notes on a piccolo
string harmonies of sounding whales
crashing crescendos of waves on rocks
lining shores of dangerous coves.

Then the gentle lapping
of tides in beaches
flying fish singing
praise the Lord
stars reflecting
wave tips of phosphorus
while mermaids
sing their haunting tunes.

My Worst Habit

My worst habit
is longing for You.
I bore my friends
to death reading
sonnets I write
about my love for You.

When You are gone
the corn in the field
ceases to grow
stars don't bother
to sparkle
the whip-or-will

grows silent
in sympathy for me.

I lose all hope
when I am not
with You
even secret medicine
cures me not.

I take only
tiny sips of air
afraid if I breathe
too deeply
I will become
the air.

You who dissolves
salt in the ocean
dissolve me
so that I might
merge with You
and never again
know this longing
for what I
already have.

No Need of Grace

How foolishly I've fought
to be independent
need pulling me
to my wants.

Finally, I realize
I need more
grace than I thought.
Finally, I am tired
of the quest I
refused to see
that I was on.

Whirlpools

I admit my wantings
to do so let's them
come, then go
not getting stuck
in a whirlpool of need.
Don't call me indecent
orgasm is the only
way I totally surrender.
Our desires are energies
that keep us moving
toward union with
the Divine.
When you do things
from your soul
it is God's grace
that fills your need.

What Exists?

If one does not
feel love in the universe
does that mean it does
not exist?

If one is blind
and cannot see the light
does only darkness exist?
A man filled with hate
has only evil ones
for neighbors.
Ah, but one whose
heart is a fountain
of love fills
the deserts with
blossoms of
unparalleled beauty.

The Skeptic

Let the thorn
expand into
the beauty of
a perfect rose.
Search for why
you exist until
you find the
book with one word
Live

Stop asking questions
you have the answer
to all
Love

Sit down on
yonder rock
and stay there
until you know
how to do both.

That Which You Are

He who praises
others, praises
himself as well.

He who criticizes
another sees only
the faults of himself.

A stick from an oak tree
cannot bear a rose.
You must be
that which you are.

Knowledge to Wisdom

The answer to "why?"
does not become clear
proportional to the number
of ties you ask.
Crossing confusion
is a long and
arduous journey
a quest, really.
Easy doesn't give
you much.
Knowing comes a little
bit at a time
to allow knowledge
to mature to wisdom.

A Nut of Truth

Truth, like a nut
comes inside a shell.
We see this shell
and think we know
the truth
and in some way
are superior
to those who cannot
even perceive the shell.

Trying to know spiritual
secrets is like trying
to drink the ocean
even little sips
are too salt.

Awe is the healer
of arrogance.

Stay away from mazes
their twists and turns
will lead you further away.
Instead, walk the labyrinth
which always takes you
to your center core.

He who walks from
his center is calm, deliberate
unconcerned with
demolitions which are
often needed
before renovations.

Cry More

Blessed is he
who cries a lot
watering the garden
like summer rains.
He whose tears glisten
on his cheeks knows
the sun will come
and grow the flowers
watered by he who
cries rain-tears
from both sadness
and joy.

A Wave

Each wave belongs to the ocean.
It rises, rises, rises
and rolls back into its Source.
It does not feel jealous
of other waves
some rising more
some less.
Each wave is what
it is and seeks
nothing but to return
from which it came.
Be a wave.

Other Worlds?

There is no "other world"
I know only what I've experienced.
If what you experience is different
is one of us in illusion?
What is an illusion
but someone else's reality?
Maybe all is real
perhaps nothing it.
Either way, it doesn't matter
for I only know
what I've experienced
the rest is contemplation.

The Pond

The only real peace
comes with I'm alone with God.
It is then that my soul unfolds
one petal at a time
becoming a sacred lotus blossom
floating on God's
pond of perfection.

Love's Sanctuary

I am in love's sanctuary
Looking at love with love.
I see what I expect to see.
I am in love's sanctuary.
I cannot take a step

forward or backwards
Nor do I need to.
I am in love's sanctuary
Looking at love with love.

My Star

You are my star
all others are
but reflections
of Your beauty.

I cannot live without You
always is not enough.
How can I visit myself?
I am a child of this moment
promises of tomorrow
are silent to me.

Only your love
can set me free
without, I am
like a ghost
without a house
to haunt.

Your Intuition

Pay attention to your
intuition, if it does
not feel right, it's not.
What is intuition
but that guidance Divine
which speaks to your soul?

But how do I know
intuition from desire?
Intuition is free of wants
it has the clarity
of a crystal bell.
It is a gift from Source.
Do not soil it with desire
and it will remain
forever pure.

Trains

We watch the train
moving past our train
and feel that we are
moving, too
yet remain still
not coming
not going
trapped in illusion
realities shifting
leaving us buffeted
not knowing
the answer to our dilemma.

Soul

Soul
ethereal, divine, eternal
universal consciousness
capable of infinite love
Co-creator

Right Here

Here I stand
in the midst of chaos
thought traffic filled
with clanging noise
paralyzed by options
none of which are good.
Those who feed on nectar
become honey
dung beetles consume
what they become.

Throne of Contemplation

The throne of contemplation
where the best poems are written
soul wisdom created
by expulsion of that not needed.

Weaving Moonbeams

I am a frog of the water
no wings do I have
yet I soar
waving moonbeams
into light-filled clouds
of the night.

Some mysteries
cannot be explained

only experienced
after which
no explanation
is needed.

Only With You

I close my lips
to open my heart.
I shut my eyes
not to be distracted
by beauty.
I inhale deeply
filling my soul
with Your presence
the aroma of Your love.
No longer do I sleep
as I jealously savor
Your nearness, unwilling
to lose even a moment
of my awareness of you
all around me.
Should I sleep even
for a little while
I dream I am an empty jar
floating in the sea
with rain all around
but never a drop
to quench my thirst
for You.

Lumber Jacks

When two lumberjacks

take the ends of the saw
they back and forth begins.
Slowly at first
even a little awkward
until they hit their stride.
Then in perfect harmony
a give and take with
balance and precision.
What a beautiful sight to see
until you finally understand
their aim is to fell the tree.

Why do we strive so hard
to become really good
at destruction?

A Surge

A surge
washed me
beyond dying
into the real beauty
of creation.

There is no way
to say
what is all around
waiting to be seen
by eyes of love.

Your Trophy

I am not your trophy
nor your possession.

My love does not give
you the right to control me.
Unconditional love does not
mean accepting unacceptable
behavior.

Love gives
not takes.

Chord of Longing

The chord of longing
keeps me attached to you
although I do not yet
comprehend its end point.
I walk with a jaunty stride
knowing you protect me
down into a pit I fall
though I saw it was there.
What about my protection?
I splutter.
"I gave you eyes
and a mind
to protect but
you used neither."
I climbed out of the pit
continued my journey.
This time using
my protection.
What a team are we!

Language With No Words

Slowly I am learning
the language that
has no alphabet
no words or sounds.
The language of wisdom
is full of spaciousness
riding on wind currents
with no wings.
I need no lips, nor voice
to speak the sacred word
Love
for it is a word of action
being
feeling
giving
Silent true
love, love
LOVE

Holding Truth

Be
B
E
like tongs these two
letters grip truth
holding it firmly
B-truth-**E**
The task seems simple
but is hard to do.
BE
It is the only way to learn
what is true.

Let Go

I was filled
with shoulds and don't
overflowing with
goals and ambition.
Why do we insist
that status quo
is wrong, even lazy?
Even surrender
requires action.
Ah, but letting go
allows stillness
and in the quiet
there is a knowing
a serenity
beingness that
needs nothing more.

Pure Water

Underground rivers
flowing in the veins
of our Mother.
Pure water circles
the globe silently
bringing life to all.

Above, snow melts
and raindrops
fill rivers that
spill into the sea
or sink into the earth
returning to underground
waterways
renewing life
again and again.
Pure water
more precious
than gold
or oil
yet squandered
at the cost
of life.

The Throne

A chair is not a throne
until a king sits on it.
Do not call yourself
a Muslim, Christian, Jew
or any other label
for without love
you'll never be able
to sit upon the Throne.

Everywhere

I'm here
yet there
I'm every where

when I am merged
with You

A Mote

A mote floating on the wind
sees the world
from a different
point of view
than the ant
crawling on the ground.

They argue endlessly
about the size
of a grain of sand
each sure that he
is right
so the story ends
in disharmony.

I've often wondered
at my need to convince
another how wrong
he must be.

I argue on and on
until the grain of sand
is washed into the sea.

Hiding in Shadows

We're afraid
so hide in the shadows
not understanding
that the only safe place
is in the Light.

Trust in the Lord

I keep saying I trust
in the Lord
yet feel afraid
at times.

Is this a lack of faith
or gentle reminder
that He is always
by my side?
I need only
call His name.

God Is

Different languages
doctrines, spiritual practices
but only one God
Creator of all
regardless of how we
try to separate Him
as we separate others
with our arrogance, indifference, hate.

How narrow is the fantasy
we create, how painful
are its results.

There is only God
all else is him, too.
A truth that will not change
regardless of how many
wars, borders, religions
man creates.
He has not impact
on God.

God Is

Freedom of Light

The light cannot sit in darkness
Darkness can't swim on land, nor birds fly in the sea.
The light cannot sit in darkness.
The choice is yours to make
But remember only in light are you free.
The light cannot sit in darkness.
Darkness cannot abide in the light.

Language of Love

Use unsayable words
without sound
not even letters
with which to write.

Speak these words
in silence

and only to those
who know
for there is much power
in them that some
wish to steal.

We think we know
their meaning but
we know nothing
of their power.

They are the language
of love:
gratitude
laughter
compassion
surrender

So Simple

There is no place
nor time
to stop saying
giving
or being love
so simple
that it seems difficult.

Love
say it
give it
be love

Choosing

You can do anything
if you so choose
Just remember that both
have consequences
that should be considered.
Freedom is seldom free
the piper must be paid
Just be sure
the price is worth it.

Many Ways

Countless ways
endless days
You show your
love for me
In return I whine
beg for more
complain about
this and that
feel adrift
like a boat
far from shore.

How patient is
Your love
always steadfast
and true
guiding me
as I slowly
merge with You.

Shared Worry

Alas, I ran out of things
to worry about.
What should I do?
I know, I'll take some
of yours, then
you can worry more, too.

Be You

I wasn't a very good Christian
was not born a Jew
I tried on various other religions
all were, too tight, didn't fit
that's it, I'm through.

Next I tried being of
American of Irish/English decent, no luck.
Even politics didn't work for me
that was a failure, too.

I asked God
Who am I?
He said
You only need to be you.

Timber!

Don't shout "Timber"
when the great tree falls
an ax murderer
doesn't yell
about his deed.

Trees are falling
all over the world.
Their screams can
be heard to the sea..
Soon, all will be desert
not even a shadow
will be found
not even you and me.

Ice Cream Cone

Ice cream cone
on a summer day
I want to savor it
but it melts away.
So I gobble it up
and feel disappointed
when its gone.
Wish I could think
of another way.
I know, I'll eat two!

Who Are You?

You are thousands
You are One
divided into stars
without number
grains of sand
universes extending
beyond the limits of time

You are eternal
all that is
is within You
yet You are so much more

Awake, Yet Asleep

I am awake, yet asleep
moving through dreams
of past and yet to be.
Images swirl
intermingling
with dread, fear
hope, joy
plucking each emotion
like a violin out of tune.

What are these nocturnal
fantasies, other dimensions
unresolved stories
from the past
hopes for the future?

They come even in the day when
I am awake, yet asleep
soul searching for what
I do not know.

Which?

The one I'm after
is after me.
Am I before
or is he?

Do I follow
or always lead
or am I just a seed?

I run away
but am still here.
He's far away
but always near.

Can't Decide

To not decide
is also a decision.
You cannot run away
from yourself.
No matter where you go
you're still there.

Rich Man

You are everywhere
yet I long for you.
I am drowning
yet thirsty.

I gaze at the stars
and wish for the sun.
Throughout the day
I plead for the night.

There is no salt in my bread
birds sing and I hear
only silence.

I am incomplete
a shadow without
a body to follow.

My eyes are open
yet my heart remains closed
thus I am a rich man
who dies in poverty.

One or Two?

I am inside looking
out through his eyes
yet I am outside
watching
wondering
how to draw the line.

Where do I stop
and he begins?
And I his twin
his shadow?
Perhaps I am, he
and he is me.
Could this be?

At Last

Let me feel you enter me
my limbs, lips tingle
with your touch.
I inhale your essence
and long for more.

The very cells of my body
melt into You
merging completely
at last.

Soon

Not quite ready yet
But soon, Lord, soon.
Gonna' give up my greed and jealously
Not quite ready yet
Gonna' lay down my burdens
Repent and do right
Not quite ready yet
But soon, Lord, soon.

Jumpin' and a Hoppin'

I be a walkin' and a talkin'
jumpin' and a hoppin'
swayin' and sashshayin'
Listenin' to the angels sing

Gonna' ride that train to glory
Gotta' laugh and tell my story
I'm changing my ways
to see better days
Safe in the arms of my Lord

Ark of Mystery

The ark of mystery
holding possibilities
for all time.
He who enters
leaves this world
forever
becoming endless
cycles of discovery.

The Stallion

The stallion rides the wind
strides of muscle
wings of passion
carries him beyond
the stars and moon

Myths of old
stories told
to each generation
Epic battles
lost and won
the hero rides
into the sun
following the Light
into the Great Beyond

A Purple Feather

Why are there
no purple feathers?
I've searched far and wide.

If only I had a purple feather
my life would be complete
I'd finally understand.

Ah, that life was so simple
"if-only's" paved the way
No matter what happens
my purple feather
would surely save the day.

Diamonds of Love

Hambone, split pea soup
on a winter day
Grandma's secret recipe
I still remember today
Memories are tiny diamonds
scattered along the way.

Trapped

Trapped by expectation
bound by desire
shackled by fear
man accepts enslavement
terrified of freedom
opportunities pass him by.

Until one day
he walks into the shadow
of a sunbeam
a fleeting glimpse
of what could be
in the world of eternity.

His transformation

is slow, a little
at a time
yet there's no
turning back
once he began.

Impolite

Not polite for women to whistle
always carry a clean handkerchief
sit with your knees together
remember to say, "Please and thank-you."
I learned the rules at my mother's knee
how to act in polite society
yet at the end of this life
I know I never fit into the role
of mother and a wife.

I'm not kidding, not jokin'
always been too out spoken.

Walk Away

Walk away
sometimes it's best
it's about control anyway.

What is this need to control?
Makes us feel better than
superior for awhile
until that niggly feeling
being less than creeps back
filling us with fear
a sense of loss

of being in a world
where power is the golden ring
that too easily slips away
and we remain a tiny mouse
shouting "here kitty, kitty!"

To No Avail

He has looked everywhere
to no avail
not understanding
he is that which he seeks.

If he could look within
any one cell
finger, toe, heart
if he would stop
fantasizing about what
he's missing, let go
of all the wrong guesses
be reborn to a clear view
he would see that for
which he longs.

The angels, who have
this knowing bow when
he passes
but still he can not
believe that voice within
that says "I *am* God."

There is no reality but Him.

Love to Talk

Oh, how we love to talk
about the troubles of the world.
One person tells a sad story
the next person has to top it.

They pass the fountain
with clear water
and drink from a muddy stream.

We are listeners
as well as speakers.
It's not enough to be silent.
If we stay to listen
we are companions
to those who fill the air
with clashing symbols of woe.

Don't Ask

We go into the fire
thinking it is the fountain of truth.
The fire whispers, drink my
sweet water, ignore the sparks.
We burn away
not understanding
that fire and water
are the same
when you are
One with All.

The Same

Can pain and comfort
be the same
There is a ringing
in my ears
that sounds like
angels singing.

A knife of pain
cuts the outer shell
allowing the lotus blossom
to open its thousand
petals of grace.

A mother in childbirth
knows each pain
pushes the baby forward
her milk draws close
ready to feed new life.

So Impatient

How impatient am I
gobbling down a morsel
while longing for the feast.

If you've been starving
you cannot eat everything
at once or it will surely return.

How forgetful I am
so many times You
whisper in my ear
yet the words seem

to slide out the other side
leaving me longing
once again.

This Love

I bow to your shadow
whisper to your cheek
my mouth pretending
for it is your lips I seek.

I squint for fear
all will see the passion
in these betraying eyes
yet they laugh and
call me a fool.

Well, fool I am
for not a breath
do I take that
does not have your name.

This love, this longing
I have compels me
consumes
completes
my soul
showing me finally
the object of this passion
is a close as the pure
love energy flowing through
us all in web of eternity.

Feeding the Flame

Finally there is no news
just the same old stories
told again and again.
Of course, that's always been true
but we're just now understanding this.

Yet we continue to follow leaders
with no integrity
buy products designed
to depopulate the Earth
live sluggish lives
consuming resources
at unsustainable rates
until we wither in
corrupt medical schemes
and wonder why
someone else does
not solve these problems.

Today, I will make a difference
no matter how small
pick up a piece of litter
smile at someone I pass by
refrain from gossip
speak only the truth
visit a sick friend.

Even small acts
multiplied by us all
will start the chain reaction
to a world where
all have value
hope flourishes
and love feeds the flame.

Private Hints

What are poems
but private hints
slivers to ponder

Don't worry about
what the poet meant
let the words
take you where they will.

Each work of art
tells a new story
to all who seeks its wisdom.

Empty

I became empty
not needing anything
filled to the brim am I
for love can only fill
an open waiting space.

Learning Patience

I am impatient
to learn how to be patient
hurry up, teach me!

The Drum

A poem is a drum
beating the rhythms of love.
Even celebrate priests
here its call.
Love is the only reality.

There's Only Love

I must laugh, clap, sing
whirl like a dervish.
I used to be respectable
a long time ago
now monkeys come to
play with me.

I am filled with echoes
daisies dot my hair
my lips are full of poetry
my heart holds
the well-known secret
there is only love
and that is You.

Infinite

How many times
can you divide
eternity?
Holographs repeating
in reflecting mirrors
spirals of endless
universes

how big is forever?

My mind cannot fathom
what my soul knows is true.
There is no end to eternity.
There's only infinite You.

Coming Home

Waiting for Your call, Lord.
eager to come home.
It's been a good life
but I'm tired
and miss You so
even though I know
You are always with me
still I'm ready
for You to call me home.

No Green

Born unable to see green
through it hangs from
every branch, I see
not a leaf of green.

Poets write sonnets about it
songs, quests, tales of heroes
who know green
that I've never seen.

How can one not see
what is all around?
Is my heart too closed

my eyes somehow
too full of other things?

If only I could see green
I am sure my life would
have meaning
and I would no longer
be a fool who can not
see what everyone else
declares is real.

More Poetry

Love has filled me
with poetry, an unstoppable
flow of proclamation
line after line
sometimes with rhyme
often stream of consciousness
blather from one drunk
on love-wine
tossing out poem after
poem declaring love
is all there is
beyond the limits of time.

Counting Time

Counting years becomes
impossible as they blur
with time, months becoming
minutes and then disappear
as memory hides all
but a few kept to

savor then they, too
disappear leaving
a soul without
an identity.

Going Away Party

The taking of one's life
is considered a sin
sick, selfish
yet what if this was
the only way death came?

Would we live our lives
differently if we had
to decide when and how
we were to die?

Would some want to
live forever, others finding
life too hard, leave early?

Death, the great equalizer
no wars, killing of any kind
crime up or down?
Illness linger forever
or not even exist in bodies
not programmed to die?

Come to my going away party
celebrate the good times
and the bad.
Then I'll quietly slip away
into the next reality
that each creates.

We write our own destiny.

Little Puff

Little twig thrown
into the fire
I'm but a puff of smoke.

Don't make me out to be
something I'm not
a puff to you
is all I need to be.

Filled with Poetry

Love has filled me
with poetry
no longer respectable
I dance on table tops
drunk, chanting poems
clapping and singing
throwing caution
to the wind.

I'm in love, in love
with You
in love with my love
for You
holding echoes
in my heart
making chains of daisies
for my hair
becoming unbearably
silly to those who

do not yet know
how love makes us all
a fool, a happy, happy fool.

A Melody

Do not play the reed.
Let each note become you.
The flute is but an instrument
of your conception.

Don't listen to the music
be the melody
notes running here and there
joyously skipping across
the score
little children
laughing at life
riding notes among the stars
content to be
a melody.

Critter Salad

Organic vegetables
means sharing my
salad with critters
I prefer not to eat.
It is hard to be
vegetarian
eating organic salads
along the way.

A Drop

A drop in the sea
Too many to count are we
Yet all are part of Thee

What Did You Say?

In Portuguese
the word for coconut and feces
is the same
making it risky
to eat my favorite cookies.

Language is full of tricks
no wonder we fail
to understand.
One needs a sense of humor
to talk in another land.

Nope!

No, no, no
the best word
if you are three
and want to drive
your parents mad.

Closer to God

Some think that because
they sit on a mountain top
they are closer to God
than he who is in the valley.

Some live on leafless lands
with endless stars overhead.
Others nestle within giant florestas
where rain falls in torrents every day.

Which does God favor?

Is God really so limited
playing favorites
one against the other
or could it be our need
to be chosen, to be jealous
lest God loves someone
else more?

Multiple gods, or a god
with limits cannot exist
except in the illusions
of men who have
yet to understand
it is we who place
limits on our perceptions
not yet ready to see
with our heart and
an open hand.

Already Are

What you seek
you already have
no need to travel
to exotic lands.
What you seek
cannot be taught by others
lay down your books
leave your guru
you already are
what you seek to become.

Circle of Darkness

A circle of darkness with light around the edges
Is the darkness coming or going?
A circle of darkness
Or is the darkness spreading outward?
A circle of darkness
With light around the edges.

The Whisperer

An old vulnerability
has returned to whisper
its lure, what I thought
was dead has raised its ugly head.

You think that dragons don't fly
that magic is just trickery.
Have you never seen evil
masked as good?

I call São Miguel
to surround me
to guard my soul
protect me form
that which seeks
to consume.

To Him do I surrender
the Creator to whom
all concede, returning
to the Light
when the work is done.

Dividing Line

I did not meet you along the way
discover you in some remote hide away
How can I find what was never lost?

I cannot love You
without loving me
where does one draw the line
between us?

The Gift of Pain

I am the pain
is a wave not
part of the sea?

Is pain my tormentor
or teacher?
I must decide

from moment to moment.

Celestial Music

There is a celestial hum
underlying my consciousness.
I move inside of it
letting it fill me
full of emptiness.

I turn, turn, turn
revolving around
stars, planets, rainbows
wrapped in moonbeams
filled with emptiness
of all knowing.

The Same

Where is the separation
between the mind and soul?
Is the consciousness
I perceive, my soul
as viewed by my mind.

How can I go
to where I already am
Can I net see
the me in you?

Baby crawling on the floor
toothless old man in diapers
the same on different
parts of the circle.

The light from the moon
is a reflection from the sun
just as I am a mirrored
light of you.

Beliefs

Belief is not required
when truth is proclaimed.
What is belief, anyway
mercurial hope
wishful thinking
accepting someone else's ideas.

Then again, truth has its
flexibilities, too.

God Is

Going down
or is it up
perhaps left
maybe right
yet always
remain where I am.

'Tis the echo that reverberates
across the hills and valleys
not I who shouts my name.

Although planets revolve
around the sun
this fiery star moves

within the swirl
of the universe.

Everything moves
yet I remain where I am
creating, my thoughts
forming dreams of realities.

God is

Lies in Layers

Don't need a costume for Halloween
Going just as I am
Layered in masks, you'll never know me
Don't need a costume for Halloween
Lies in layers
Life is all pretend
Don't need a costume for Halloween
Going just as I am

What Is Spirituality?

What is spirituality
a quest?
exclusive club?
a huge money maker, for sure.

Why do I fill page after page?
Why do you read these words?
Can you come here
and sit in silence with me?

Can you look in my eyes

exchanging, loving
receiving, giving
without expectation?

Become me
while I become you
until finally we understand
there is only One.

Nothing More

I am not going to do
anything today
accomplish nothing
not even going to
feel guilty about it.

I've let go of goals
desires, even hope is useless
learned how to sit in the sun
lie in the shade
sleep when it come
eat when I'm hungry.

No longer waiting
or longing
seeking, or praying.
I'm just am being
what I am
and nothing more.

Inside of Walls

Cities where people

live inside of walls
locks, alarms
CCTV
embedded tracking microchips
no more land of the free.

Darkness is covering
all in its path
an era preceding the end
filled with chaos.

Yet I remain in serenity
understanding it doesn't
matter how the story ends
for there is only You.

And Then There Is

Blindness leads to visions
deafness is filled with music celestial
silence replaces endless chatter
until there is only
the essence of being.

I Exist

If you take a photo of me
I will not be there
an embrace finds
only empty air.

Yet I exist
I am
will be

forever

Power of Intention

I n all we say our soul is revealed
N o one is harmed more than he with mal-intent
T ruth shines through
E ach intention becomes its reality
N ever is good intention wasted
T ime is often needed for good intentions to manifest
I ntention is the fuel of action
O ur intentions create
N ever decide without knowing your intention

Face

F eatures marked by time
A mask does not change who you are
C haracter outlined by creases
E ach face has its own beauty

Face2

I cannot face
the face in the mirror
lying to one's self
fools the fool

Face3

About face
return to face
the consequences
of your double face

Face4

Face that haunts me
follows me
whispering what
I try to deny.

Go away, I demand
not yet admitting
the face is mine.

Calling Forth

Swans and dragons
mystical balls of light
sorcery on a summer night
calling forth all to see
beyond this life
into the world
of eternity

Disco Queen

Disco queen with painted lips
strobe lit forms moving intermittently
a night of ecstasy
ending when the rooster crows
and she returns to her reality

Childhood Stories

top hat
crazy cat
eating ham and eggs
story unfolds
to children of old
Dr. Suess generation
has gotten old

and I who read
these stories endless
to my children
remember fairy tales
of Grimn realities

Finger and Thumb

We are morphing into
a head with no brain
and a body with only
a finger and thumb
tapping endlessly

U R

U R
A generation
of abbreviations
lol, brb
as soon as I figure out
what u said

True Serenity

Only when we realize
that we are
always have been
forever will be
United with the core
of our Creator
will we know
true serenity.

Having Fun

My poetry is not profound today
each line is full of simple play
yet it contains inspiration
from a God who smiles
on His creation.

Life is not to be taken
so seriously that we
forget the simple joy
of having fun.

Bird Blessings

Resurrection bird
Wet wings drying in the sun
Blesses all who pass by

A Delicacy

Eating bugs is not my fare
though people are doing it everywhere.
If I wasn't vegetarian before
Pass the salad, I want some more.

Me

My best companion is inside
this being that I call "me."
No matter how I look or act outside
my me remains just me.

Sometimes I am not kind
or thoughtful
I can be impatient, selfish, too
but this wonderful part of me
is always just what I'm supposed to be.

Excellence

I do not want excellence
that single focus needed
to master just one skill.

No gold medals do I need
the World's Greatest Nothing
do I want to be.

Let me be a jack-of-all-trades
a sampler of life
find joy in the simplest things.

Good enough is fine with me
for the many things that I enjoy.
a butterfly in God's garden
flitting from flower to flower
taking tiny sips of life
is the perfect life for me.

Just a Moment

A breath
heartbeat
sigh
moment in time
life
is as simple as this

No More Drama

D iversions of foolery

R acing to nowhere

A ction of avoidance

M aking smoke-puff problems

A drenaline junkie

Giving Thanks

Flowers plants trees vines
birds frogs snakes snails
rain sunny days misty fogs
Did I say "thank you" today?

Forever Friend

Am I as good a friend
as I want you to be?
Can you always count on me?
Do I make you laugh
hold you when you cry
believe in you
as the years go by?

Let's be forever friends
allowing our love to grow
beyond eternity.

Hiding

Am I hiding in my book
lost in stories
free of the here and now
for these hours?

Why do I feel a bit guilty
as I lie in a hammock
reading a book I enjoy?

How crazy is this?
Just another thing that
I am letting go.
as I learn the joy
of how to just be.

No Plans

After years of goals
planning far in advance
ranting affirmations
laundry list praying
I have stopped.

If something comes
I accept it
if nothing comes
that is fine, too.

Only Me

me
me, me
me, me, me
me, me, me, me

Really, who else is there?

No More Journeys

How we latch on to the "spiritual" journey

light workers, spiritual journey
enlightenment, mystical
a whole new language has evolved
just in my lifetime.

Bookshelves, Internet sites are
full of
How to Be More Spiritual
seems unnecessary when I
really think about it, though.
Goodness knows I also
jumped on this bandwagon.

But now that I've pared my life down
to a pace that allows reflection
I think I am getting rid of this
searching
journeying
thrown out longing, too

I am finding life much
more simple than we usually
let it be
think I'll keep
serenity.

New Teacher

There was a new teacher at school
who didn't know what to do
so she stood on her head
the children laughed and said
teach us to do that, too.

Drinking

I do not drink any more
nor do I drink any less
what I drink is a secret
so you'll just have to guess.

What if we released
all the people in prison
who are there because
of booze or drugs.
In their place we
put people wh instigate
profit from and participate
in war, destruction
of natural resources
contamination of our
food and water, steal
money with scams
or corruption.
Those who do harm
to animals and people.

Why are millions of dollars
spent on Olympics
while even one child
dies of hunger?

How did our values
get so askew?
It's everyone's fault
even me and you.

Wondrous Is She

Elephant's trunk can pick up a nut

monkey's tail holds onto the tree
snails carry their house on their backs
honey is made from flowers by bees.

How wondrous is nature
yet how seldom do we notice.
When was the last time
you watched the sun set
or went out to see the moon?

Blue light specials
are not needed in nature
for its beauty is free.

Anticipation

A waiting time to savor

N o need to rush

T ake the time to enjoy this pleasure

I n no rush are we

C ount your blessings first

I nvent reasons to delay

P articipate fully in the moment

A fterwards is too late

T he foreplay should not be neglected

I love these moments just before

O ne moment of appreciation

N ow, go!

Make Me Laugh

I like people who make me laugh
for I tend to be a little glum
so give me all your humor
and I will give you some, too.

More and more, I only want
to focus on what gives life joy
prophets of doom
dark tales of woe
I traded for sweet moments
that leave me grateful
to be alive.

No Jail

Clothes pin, bobby pin
safety pin, clamp
handcuffs
bars on doors
no longer free

Don't tie me up
tell me I can't
make fun if I fail.
I'm bursting out
of this prison
your jealousy
is my jail no longer.

Clatter Chatter

Making up stories
in my mind
clatter chatter
all day long

Be quiet, please
I plead
no more
a woeful deed.

How long can you go
without thinking something
negative
critical
thought of what-if?

No Proof Needed

Once we give up proof
all things are possible
science without magic
faith without love
leaves only sad illusion
and an empty heart.

Devouring Life

I am no longer devouring life
taking occasional tiny bites
savoring each as I go
making it last all day

I've even been known to fast
though that is a thing of the past

This restraint has shown me
the numbing effect of more
addicting compulsion of greed
the delight of doing with care

Awe

Single blade of grass
One petal from a bouquet
Value comes from awe

The Connoisseur

My dog is a connoisseur of treats
not just anyone will do.
He wants only certain things on my plate
and sighs with indignation
if I eat them instead of
giving him what he deems
is his rightful due.

My dog has a pet woman
that he works hard to train
little by little she's learning
but it's hard to teach
an old woman new tricks.

More and More

More money, more sex, more chocolate
more power, more control
more of everything
leaves one longing for more

Not Yet

I want to go in a bakery
take a bite of everything
go to a fancy restaurant
eat only their best dessert

Walk in a field of strawberries
eat one warm from the sun

Next I'll count the stars
naming them one by one
hug everyone I meet
laugh where I'm supposed
to cry
only then will I
be ready to die

Vanilla Me

Good thing I don't want to be perfect
Just plain, ole vanilla me
One old woman in the floresta
Just learning how to be

Just a Game

Children playing cops and robbers
soldiers going off to war
cowboys and Indians
bang, bang you're dead
has worsened to
blood and gore
violence unlimited
video games

It's just a game
is not true
our thoughts become
our reality

Let's teach our children
how to laugh, run, climb
fly kites, play with puppies
how to love, share
know the sheer joy of life

Where Is Home?

Home is where you're headed
not where you are.
Don't get too comfortable
in your rocking chair.
Know that you can be home
anywhere.

Upside Down

I walk on my hands
not my feet
blow kisses to all I meet

sing songs backwards
write silly poems
on bathroom walls

What has caused
this madness
unreasonable joy?
Love, say I
my love for You
Your love for me
shows me what life
is supposed to be.

Footsteps

Hard rock
produces no footsteps.
Leave a trail to heaven
so others may follow.
This is not a singular journey.

Icing on the Cake

Love is icing
that need no cake.
It can't be explained
for it is a state
of being that defines
logic, explanation, demands.

Love is
what it is not
as well as what
it is

But what is love?
you may well ask.
It is the answer
to the questions
you seek
the bond you have
with all you meet.

Love is you
and me.
Love is our Creator.
Love is Eternity.

Paper Airplane

Paper airplane flying high
going beyond the endless sky;

Refusing to hear that he's not real
he soars above clouds
does loopy-loops
rides air currents
with eagles
lives his dreams
of being a paper airplane
flying high.

All Day Sucker

An all-day sucker
only lasts all day
if you give only licks

He who takes big bites
becomes the sucker
without a sucker.

No Shoulds

Stop doing
what you don't want to do.
Don't let others
fill you with should
leaving only
a tombstone of regrets.

Leave this life
filled with joyous memories
of what you did
instead of regrets
for what you didn't do.

Tread With Care

Pride
arrogance
or knowing your worth
the line is thin
tread carefully

Don't Just Take

T oo many takers

A lways give more than you take

K eep the earth in balance

E ach gift is for the giver

Into the Hole

No more do I give others
power over my life
not doctors, churches
politicians
losers
mothers
neighbors who gossip
the list seems endless

Into the hole goes
should, threats, regulations
authority…another word for control
obligation, custom
my need for your approval

I have but One whom I
willingly follow
and He asks
only that I love.

Seems to cover
it all to me.

Don't Bother

Mysteries are not
to be solved.
Don't bother to ask, "why?"

Science teaches us
to question everything
religion tells us
to have faith

But I learned
what works for me
is to just accept
what is
to simply let things
be
what they are.

The Swing

She swings

                          up high

and back again

                          her squeals of delight

make my heart

                    sing

Snow Drops

Snow Drops
delicate, promising, welcomed
how relieved we are when they appear
Harbinger of Spring

Cat in a Hat

If I was a cat
I'd wear a hat not a cap
Quite chic I would be

The Rum Bum

He never uses chewing gum
it doesn't mix well with rum
his mouth doesn't work right
when he drinks rum day and night
now everyone says
he's a rum bum

Deciding

Nope
not now
maybe never
perhaps sometime
Okay, I will

When it's hard to decide
I get all panicky inside
for fear I'll do it wrong
but the truth is
all decisions are
but gates to new experiences
filled with lessons
so just decide
the one that feels right
and be open to what
you can learn.

Beautiful

B eauty starts inside
E ach of us has our own unique beauty
A llow your love to shine forth
U se the blush of kindness
T ry laughter instead of lipstick
I nclude gratitude in all you do
F ind the beauty in others
U nique is each star
L ove is what really makes us beautiful

www.ingramcontent.com/pod-product-compliance
Lightning Source LLC
Chambersburg PA
CBHW031308060426
42444CB00032B/233